A Lady In Waiting

MARTINA SIMS

Copyright © 2025 by Martina Sims

All rights reserved. This book or any portion thereof may not be reproduced or used in any manner whatsoever without the express written permission of the publisher except for the use of brief quotations in a book review.

Printed in the United States of America

First Edition, 2025

PAPERBACK ISBN: 979-8-3493-9241-2

EBOOK ISBN: 979-8-3493-9242-9

Red Pen Edits and Consulting

www.redpeneditsllc.com

TABLE OF CONTENTS

DEDICATIONS.. 1

INTRODUCTION 3

CHAPTER 1

The Prancer.. 5

CHAPTER 2

The Jealous Woman (Spirit)................................ 17

CHAPTER 3

The Praying Woman 31

CHAPTER 4

Preparation 41

CHAPTER 5

The Detox 53

CHAPTER 6

Timing.. 63

CHAPTER 7
Promise 73

CHAPTER 8
Worth The Wait 81

RESOURCES 97

ABOUT THE AUTHOR 99

DEDICATIONS

This book is dedicated to my beloved mother, Mary –

The epitome of grace, strength, and unwavering faith.

Your strength was quiet but unshakable.

You were love in its purest form - caring, supportive, and endlessly encouraging.

My first example of resilience, grace, with the kind of power that doesn't shout, but endures.

With gentle hands and a strong spirit, you pushed me into purpose, never letting me forget who I was or what I could become.

A classy lady in every sense - dignified, dignifying, and deeply inspiring.

Your legacy lives on through this book and in the empowered footsteps of every woman it touches.

This book is for you and for every woman who carries the fire forward.

INTRODUCTION

This book is about helping women identify where they are, emotionally, spiritually, or mentally. It will take a look at patterns that come along with pain. It is my prayer and hope that this book will help women become the best version of themselves. Some of us have been in the spaces mentioned throughout this book. Some of us are in this space currently while others are coming out of this space. If we are honest, we can all relate to what will be discussed. It is my hope that we can find ourselves in the script. In order to find yourself in the script, there has to be a mirror. The mirror can be someone else's testimony, a book, a person, or experiences that helped us reflect and take the necessary steps to become a better version of ourselves. The late Michael Jackson said it best: *"I'm starting with the man in the mirror. I'm asking him to change his ways."* Once you see yourself in the script, you are on your way to change for the better. This is where it all begins - with you recognizing the issue. Are you ready for change?

CHAPTER 1

The Prancer

A Prancer is a behavior or Spirit (lust), that operates through a woman who has been wounded, abandoned, overlooked, rejected, going through a breakup, and the list goes on. This chapter will explain how a woman has reached a level in her pain that affects her decisions which in turn, influences her actions. Those actions ultimately affect her life. She is one who is impatient with waiting on God. Her emotions have taken her to a place of anxiousness. She becomes so impatient that she takes matters into her own hands. She takes extreme measures to be noticed by men. Her mannerisms begin to change, especially in the presence of men who are taken. The depth of the pain and hurt cause's her to feel undesirable and unwanted. She feeds off of taken men due to single men not giving her the time of day. She has experienced rejection from the men she once loved which caused pain. The glance of a taken man does her heart good. She feels seen and powerful in that moment. That glance fuels her behavior even the more.

There are levels to her pain. This level of pain causes her decisions to be emotionally led. When a woman is emotionally led, her emotions run rampant, and she doesn't make sound decisions. It can lead her down a path of becoming known as "The Prancer". The Prancer loves being seen. She's been ignored and rejected by men for so long that she may not even be fully aware of her actions. On some levels, she is doing what is referred to as fueling. She is paying other women back for what she has gone through or what has been done to her. The prancer is known as an attention-seeker.

I've worked in the cosmetology industry for many years which has allowed me to listen to countless stories of women dealing with pain. We, as women, need each other more than we know. That's why the enemy loves division as well as discord. The more we are divided, the more we will miss the opportunity to share common experiences that will help one another. One of the reasons I loved being a full-time hairstylist was the ability and opportunity to help women. I did this by building their self-esteem. I was able to build their interior while beautifying their exterior. I loved on them despite what they shared. This is imperative for communities of women that seek to be there for one another. The community will tell you when you're off and nourish you back to health (spiritually, mentally, and emotionally).

The Prancer's behavior stems from loneliness, rejection, insecurity, breakups, low esteem, low confidence, being overlooked, mistreatment, and more. This woman is sometimes at her wits' end with waiting and desiring love. She feels unseen and undesired by men. The moment she receives an inclination of attention, whether from a married or taken man, lust begins to fuel her. Deception creeps in and she begins to believe that her actions are justified. Her actions and motives become more obvious. Her insecurities are masked in confidence out loud, but it's still insecurity. The Prancer becomes envious of couples/marriages because they have what she wants. One of the biggest lies that fuel this behavior is to think that your life is with someone else's husband or that the man will be better with you than his significant other. Some have gone as far as to emulate the wife/woman by studying her style. In this phase, the prancer has lost her identity and self-worth. She begins to stoop so low that there is nothing that she won't do to get the life she feels she deserves. It's a life she feels she has been robbed of. She's tired of not being chosen, being overlooked, and feeling undesired. In this season of her life, the enemy dangles relationships in her face as a reminder that she's single, alone and unwanted. Can I remind you that you are never alone. God will never leave you nor forsake you (Hebrews 13:5). The enemy has deceived her to believe that the attention from married or taken men was the confidence needed to get back out on the dating scene. The only attention shes attracted to after this door is open, is from someone who is already taken. The more attention given, the more the pain is masked.

Looking from the outside, she is confident and desirable to those who can't see it. However, for those who can, we see right through it. The Prancer begins to do things that are completely out of character and sometimes, embarrassing. The embarrassment is sometimes noticed after healing. A wise woman once said: "What you attract when you're hurt, you'll be disgusted by when you're healed. The Prancer shows up in different settings with the intent to gain married or taken men attention. From parties, clubs, gatherings, even church settings; The Prancer likes to flaunt her stuff at opportune times when all eyes are on her. The Prancer looks for places and opportunities to be seen by married and taken men. Some Prancers go as far as trying to get a reaction out of the wife or significant other. They seek loopholes in the relationships as a way in. This pain is so deep that she's willing to hurt another woman although she has experienced the same pain. I've been in many settings where there is at least one Prancer present. One of the best decisions you can ever make is take time for yourself and heal. When you are healed, you see clearly and will attract differently. If you don't, this can be you. The job of the enemy is to get you so far out in the deep to destroy you. I've heard stories of people when they were under the influence of alcohol and not being sober-minded. They told how they couldn't remember what had happened the day before. Someone had to tell them. Once told, they had to come to the realization that what was done was embarrassing. When pain isn't addressed or dealt with, staying in that place will eventually embarrass you. This behavior can show up through many doors. We talked about it being due to rejection, not being chosen and other areas of pain. Another doorway is through the ear and eye gates. I'm reminded of this woman who was my neighbor at the time. When she first moved beside me, I noticed her car was scratched up. I heard this still, small voice telling me it was because of infidelity. After settling in, my neighbor and I had a general conversation where she introduced herself. Shortly after she introduced herself, she just blurted out, "Yeah, someone keyed my car when I went back home." She further began to tell me about how she's with a married man she met. She explained when she met him and how she felt justified in being with him. Her story even contained talking bad about the wife whom she has never met. She explained how she was banking where he and his wife banked and the wife found out. She was so confident and comfortable in her sharing. By sharing this, it pretty much confirmed her car being scratched up, was indeed due to infidelity! It was confirmation for me. Over time, I observed this same neighbor begin getting in the ear of another neighbor. This other neighbor was really sweet and conservative and normally stayed to herself. I remember all of a sudden her going from conservatively dressed to dressing completely out of her element. I noticed the same spirit were now operating through her. I sensed the nice neighbor was extremely lonely. Loneliness invited that spirit in. She began to prance at the mere presence of a man. When men would come around, she would flirt in very subtle but noticeable ways. One day, she asked my guy to look at her daughter's car when I wasn't home. Although she was very sweet, she had never spoken to me or my guy. We never communicated or had a conversation. She was looking for an open door in our relationship. She looked like a deer in headlights when I pulled up. I immediately asked her, "How can I help you?". She began to over explain all while looking guilty. Her face told it all! She didn't want my help…she had motives. She couldn't face me from that day forward because her plans failed. She had allowed the new neighbor to get into her ear gate. She was told the benefits of being with someone else's man. What she didn't know was, that same lady who got in her ear, would share with me how nothing was working for her. Everything she tried failed and she felt cursed. It's just like the enemy to not let you in on the consequences that come with your actions. The neighbor, who could no longer face me, became someone totally out of character. The Prancer was invited in her life through loneliness and allowing someone into her ear gate. The Spirit of lust was so strong within her that she even began to dress like me in attempt to get what she wanted. Whatever hairstyle I would wear, I noticed that she would change her hair to mimic the same.. She had lost her identity and began to emulate me…even down to my mannerism. Her thought process became: "She dresses this way so it must be what he likes." That thought led her into trying to conform in hopes of capturing his attention. I share this story for many reasons. One being, she allowed someone to catch her ear which caused her to stumble. It also caused her to suffer embarrassment. The Word asks: *"Who did hinder you that ye should not obey the truth."* (Galatians 5:7). The nice neighbor mentioned to me that she was a believer in Christ on the day she asked my guy to look at her daughter's car. I showed grace but not stupidity. I served that Spirit notice immediately.

I had already written this chapter of this book in 2012. For me to encounter the very thing given to me to write about, was a preparation in knowing how to respond. That encounter was in 2023. It's amazing how the Lord will prepare you for such a time as this. The book was written in a notebook in 2012. Through the toll of doing hair, I was ready to encounter so many women plus reach the masses. I dare not conclude this chapter without giving some tools to help you not become The Prancer.

A LADY IN WAITING

The first advice would be when you're wounded, Detox. (I will explain in a later chapter.) Detox from relationships and focus on your healing. Be careful what and who you're listening to. Feed yourself the Word to build you and your confidence. Use affirmations to declare over yourself. Go places that add to your mental health. Love you like you loved that someone, or how you would desire to be loved. Surround yourself with optimistic people, settings, and positive influences. Don't come off detox until you feel the need not to settle! Although I disagree with the choices others make that got them or led them to this place, I understand.

While writing this book, I happened to be watching the Tamron Hall Show. The P-Valley Star, Nico, was explaining a new show where people pretty much lived some of the characters' lives, in real life. I happened to watch a clip of the show. The young lady in the show is a dancer. Her children's father died in a car accident, which left her to provide for the children. The job she had wasn't enough to make ends meet. It's easy to quickly judge without knowing someone else's story. The Prancer is merely a wounded woman searching for attention. It doesn't justify her actions, however, in the end, the other woman is in the relationship or marriage. You don't know what she's been through to have the relationship that she has. To have a man who adores her. She, too, could've been wounded and finally gotten her happily ever after. I remember being a part of this ministry. I was fairly new and just getting out of a relationship. Of course, the enemy dangled what appeared to be a healthy relationship in my face. Remember, whatever you believe in, will be dangled in your face as a way to discourage you. It could be the wanting of a house, car, child, spouse, job, peace, or joy. Whatever it is, it's like it becomes magnified. This means you began to see more people with what you believe for more than usual. I can remember one day watching a couple as they were headed into the building. The male held the door and smiled at the woman with admiration. I said: "Aww, I can't wait to have someone like that." At this time, I was around 24 or 25 years of age. She looked at me, chuckling as she walked into the building. Later on that evening, she called me on the phone. I had no idea how she got my number, let alone my name. She began to introduce herself and repeated my comment from earlier. She proceeded to tell me to be careful what I ask for because her husband had HIV. She went on in detail as to how he contracted the disease, which was from sleeping around. He slept around throughout the last few year's of their marriage. She stated that the Lord told her to stop sleeping with him years ago and was glad she listened. She shared that due to her profession as a Nurse and her personal health, she had to be tested often.The moral of the story is you maybe prancing to get what you think another woman has and not realize what you're asking for. From that day forward, I've never looked at life the same. I began to measure my life based on where the Lord had brought me from instead of comparing it to others. Comparison kills.

CHAPTER 2

The Jealous Woman (Spirit)

Jealousy can be dangerous. I've experienced this so much that it has become my norm. I remember my mom staring at me once and whispering, *"Baby, you scare me because you remind me so much of me."* People are going to hate you just because your shoes match your shirt. I was around 9 or 10 at the time. I looked at her like, huh?! She knew the road ahead. Boy, was she right! I've experienced this throughout life. From being jealous of how I was shaped, to my humor, genuine heart, inner and outer beauty, intelligence, talents, and just how others loved or liked me. This is one of the biggest reasons why people may lie on you, so that others can see you negatively. There is nothing new under the sun. This has been happening from the beginning of time - Cain and Abel days. I've experienced this in every setting, from people close to me, the church setting, business settings, professional settings, gatherings, and functions. You name it.

I like to call it extreme jealousy and twisted admiration. Twisted admirers start off admiring you from afar, only to try to get close to see what they can find out about you that's gossip-worthy. Once they're up close and personal, they realize that you're really a dope person. They become offended because you're more than just surface, and more than what meets the eye. They are even more mad and jealous that there is nothing to report back to the enemy's camp.

Jealousy comes in all forms. I will deal with a few here. Twisted admirers are surface people. They have the "if I can't beat them, join them" mentality. This means that they have a conscious and they may be willing to change. Sometimes, they can encounter someone to love on them, to fill that love deficit, and change takes place. They may have lacked love and confidence and just needed a boost to get on track with life.

The extremely jealous woman is dangerous. This spirit that operates through this woman is evil.

The extremely jealous woman (spirit) wants to cause bodily harm. In a matter of seconds, my mom would see right through these types of people. There are two parts to the extremely jealous woman. This spirit wants to be you. She mimics everything about you: the way you wear your hair, the way you dress, your style. This woman will go to extreme measures to be you and harm you. This woman hates you but wants to be around to get the updates on you. Remember, everything about this spirit is extreme. Do not underestimate this spirit. Everything that you think it will do, it will. The second part to this extremely jealous woman is even more evil. I remember when I moved into this apartment. One of my neighbors introduced herself to me. She asked if she could decorate my place. Under different circumstances, it would have been a big fat "No!". I don't allow anyone in my home. I had just come out of a busy season, so I was not vigilant. This is why it is so important to get rest. Your vision is clear, and you're able to make sound decisions. I told her yes. She told me that she decorated for Marci from the news station. I knew that I was dealing with a liar because everybody knew our local news anchor, Darci Strickland. I said, "Do you mean Darci Strickland?"

She said, "Yeah, her lol". Although I was tired, I still discerned something wasn't right. She began to tell me how much I favored her sister. My shape, complexion, and my demeanor. I thought that was a compliment. Boy, was I wrong. She proceeded to tell me that she liked to smoke marijuana and if I ever smelled it, to let her know. Days later, I smelled it, and I told her. It happened a few more times back-to-back. At this point, she got highly offended, but she told me to let her know.

I had to remember that, according to **Ephesians 6:12**, *"For we wrestle not against flesh and blood, but against principalities, against powers, against the rulers of the darkness of this world, against spiritual wickedness in high places."*

The torment began. She scratched my car every chance she got. The Lord was letting me know her scheme every time she would do something to me. She cut my cable wire right in the middle of me watching TV. When the things she tried didn't anger me, she began to do more. She put something in the air vents to make me choke and be sick. I remember reporting it to management. Nothing was done, so I got it in writing. I told my family that I knew she was putting something in the air vents. I stayed sick until I started counteracting in prayer.

One day, my aunt and cousins came to visit. When one of my cousins arrived, I noticed that he was talking to someone who was visiting her. The person my cousin was talking to happened to be related to my cousin. This is why you must also be careful who you mistreat. Upon walking my aunt to her car, the neighbor asked if she could speak to me. I was hesitant because now I see her for who she is and who she serves. I know from a spiritual perspective that darkness hates light. This is one of the reasons she targeted me, along with her being jealous of her sister. If she loved her sister, and I reminded her of her sister, she would have treated me better. That's what I thought. I covered myself through prayer, building a wall and a hedge of protection around me. Before I could get to her, she began to confess what she had done to me. My mouth dropped in astonishment as she told me how. She stated, "I put some stuff in the air vents to make you choke". In her words, "I was trying so hard to choke you, that it ended up choking me and my grandbaby. I had to leave my apartment for the day".

One thing about a demonic spirit is that it will tell you its mission. You must pay attention. She didn't stop there. She put black dirt where I would walk right in front of my porch and walkway. At this point, I knew this was total witchcraft. I'm dealing with a whole witch. Something happened in her life that caused her to be very jealous of women with my complexion to the point of doing witchcraft as her defense. Years prior, I remember the Lord giving me an urgency to study snakes and their operation as well as witchcraft. I had no desire to study either of them. The mere thought of both would make me quiver. I was obedient. I realized how the natural is connected to the spiritual. The python's mission is to squeeze the life out of its prey. This can be correlated to the demonic realm. I remember being tired all the time. I had no go, or strength. I couldn't complete tasks. Everything I tried failed. I wasn't prospering at all. The purpose of the black dirt was to keep me from moving out of the apartment and to torment me. Evil, pure evil. I share this because you can't take this lightly. This is demonic. According to 1 Peter 5:8, you must "Be sober, be vigilant; because your adversary the devil, as a roaring lion, walketh about, seeking whom he may devour". I knew the python was operating through witchcraft. The holy spirit reminded me of the urgency to study snakes so I would know what I was up against.

At first, I was angry. I asked the Lord, "what in the world is wrong with people that they feel the need to do such things to innocent people?" When I would pray, I would be so mad and angry because it would be a constant thing. Some would say, "why didn't you move?" The spirit of backwardness and stagnation was the enemy's mission for my life. The enemy sought to keep me broke so I wouldn't have the finances to move. I had to pull out my arsenal of targeted prayers that would dismantle this evil. The Lord knew before I moved there that I would encounter a witch. She would monitor my going and my coming. When I started to pray fervently, she would be so afraid that she would burn sage to counteract. I had to change my prayers. I would put my little spin on it by saying, "send back to sender whatever she would do to me". You haven't done anything until you've been challenged to pray for someone who has tried to destroy you.

Whew! Lord, have mercy! That is a challenge, but the moment I began to pray for her, things started to change. I prayed the word only. I prayed that the Lord would avenge me. I prayed other scriptures such as **Psalm 91**:

1 He that dwelleth in the secret place of the most High shall abide under the shadow of the Almighty.

2 I will say of the Lord, He is my refuge and my fortress: my God; in him will I trust.

3 Surely he shall deliver thee from the snare of the fowler, and from the noisome pestilence.

⁴ He shall cover thee with his feathers, and under his wings shalt thou trust: his truth shall be thy shield and buckler.

⁵ Thou shalt not be afraid for the terror by night; nor for the arrow that flieth by day;

⁶ Nor for the pestilence that walketh in darkness; nor for the destruction that wasteth at noonday.

⁷ A thousand shall fall at thy side, and ten thousand at thy right hand; but it shall not come nigh thee.

⁸ Only with thine eyes shalt thou behold and see the reward of the wicked.

⁹ Because thou hast made the Lord, which is my refuge, even the most High, thy habitation;

¹⁰ There shall no evil befall thee, neither shall any plague come nigh thy dwelling.

¹¹ For he shall give his angels charge over thee, to keep thee in all thy ways.

¹² They shall bear thee up in their hands, lest thou dash thy foot against a stone.

¹³ Thou shalt tread upon the lion and adder: the young lion and the dragon shalt thou trample under feet.

¹⁴ Because he hath set his love upon me, therefore will I deliver him: I will set him on high, because he hath known my name.

¹⁵ He shall call upon me, and I will answer him: I will be with him in trouble; I will deliver him, and honour him.

¹⁶ With long life will I satisfy him, and shew him my salvation.

I prayed **Isaiah 54:17**:

No weapon that is formed against thee shall prosper; and every tongue that shall rise against thee in judgment thou shalt condemn. This is the heritage of the servants of the Lord, and their righteousness is of me, saith the Lord.

Because witches monitor your whereabouts, they'll know how to stand against your progress. I had to speak, decree, and declare the word constantly. It is so awesome how the Lord will keep you in the know. He will reveal the enemy's devices, plot, ploy, and plan. That's why I love the Lord so much. I continued to pray that whatever caused her to be hurt and to let evil in, that she would heal. I started praying for her heart and that every time she would revolt against me, she would have an encounter face to face with the Lord.

He did it for John Ramirez, who was a satanist. He grew up learning how to be evil and how to harm people, specifically, believers of Christ. His whole family was filled with witches and warlocks. He shares his testimony all over the world. I believed the Lord could do the same for Valarie.

I moved the black dirt from my porch as instructed by the holy spirit. When I did that, she realized that I was on to her evil. The attacks were milder, but still present. The tables began to turn. She began to speak, wanted to have small talk, and realized that I wasn't her enemy. I encountered so much with her, but I made sure I was spirit-led. I moved as I was instructed with her. When the tables turned, she apologized to me. She said she didn't know why she was so mean to me. "You've never done anything to me. I am so sorry."

The Lord told me she would come back and apologize, but that didn't mean I needed to eat lunch with her. The Lord avenged me on my behalf. Extreme jealousy is so real. This is someone's reality. People want to take your spot. They have no idea what you have to go through on a day-to-day basis. They don't know what it takes to be you. I want those who encounter jealousy to know, I get it. It can be exhausting because you're just being yourself. One thing I learned is not to borrow someone else's issues. Their issue has nothing to do with you. Don't internalize it. If you have a prayer life, pull out your arsenal, the word of God, because you will need it on your journey. If I can encourage those of you who don't have a prayer life, start. I look forward to helping you on your journey. Allow this prayer to be an addition to your prayer life or the beginning of a new prayer life.

My Prayer

Father, I thank you for making me different. Lord, I thank you for protecting my heart despite of what I've experienced. I pray your fire wall and hedge of protection over me. I decree and declare according to your word in **Isaiah 54:17** *that No weapon that is* *formed against thee shall prosper; and every tongue that shall rise against thee in judgment thou shalt condemn. I thank you, Lord that vengeance belongs to you. Therefore, I trust you for you know the thoughts and plans you have for me according to* **Jeremiah 29:11***. Lord, you said to put you in remembrance of your word to perform it according to* **Isaiah 43:26***. If you said it, it is so. Lord, I thank you! Every evil altar with my name on it, break it up into irreputable pieces. May every hex, black magic, incantations, witchcraft, soothsayer, and every evil word prayer spoken over my life be renounced right now in the name of Jesus. Lord, I thank you that every monitoring spirit's eyes be blinded, and every ear be deafened. Every astral projecting operation be dismantled in the name of Jesus. I thank you that I will not fear what men can do to me. You said that perfect love casts out fear. Therefore, I rest in faith. I thank you that you haven't given me the spirit of fear but love, power, and a sound mind. Lord, go before me each day. Be my front and rear guard. Let no hurt, harm, or danger come near my dwelling. I decree and declare that the net my enemies hide will entangle them. May the pit that they dig for me consume them, and they fall in it. I plead the blood of Jesus over me,* *my family, my home, my life, my vehicle, and over my going and coming. Lord, you said to pray for my enemies. I lift my enemies before you. I ask that whatever caused them to be evil towards me may be healed. Heal the parts of them that they haven't shared with anyone. Mend their broken heart. Heal them from the trauma that caused them to project their hurt onto other people. Lord, may they encounter you in a mighty way. May they experience your love in a way that they come to know you personally. Let your love overtake them where it drives out hate, jealousy, and fear. Let your power do the work in them. I believe that I receive all that I prayed for…*

In Jesus' Name,

Amen.

CHAPTER 3

The Praying Woman

The praying woman is a reflection of God. When you pray, it reflects the heart of God. This part is very vital and shouldn't be taken lightly. Prayer is about the heart and its posture. In 1 Timothy 2:8, Paul wasn't speaking on the physical posture of prayer, but rather the position of the heart during prayer. Our posture is a reflection of how our heart responds to God. During this process, your heart's posture matters. It matters for healing, processing, and being who God has called you to be. As mentioned in previous chapters, all of this is necessary. You must learn how to pray fervently. Learning this was the best decision I made on my personal journey. It allowed me to be effective and to pray without giving up. Praying fervently means to pray with intensity and passion. The Word tells us that the effectual fervent prayer of the righteous man availeth much. What does that look like, you may be asking… It's thanking God, praying the Word, and asking the Lord for His will to be done. A praying woman must be in a position to hear clearly. She has to have her ear to the mouth of God. The Prancer and the Seductive woman are prime examples of when your prayer life slips. In His presence is fullness of joy. The moment emotions go contrary to what the Word says, is when you know its time to return to prayer. Being stuck in unhealed trauma, pain, and shame can push us away from prayer at times. When we allow prayer to be our last result, we operate like the Prancer or the seductive woman. Remember I mentioned how important it is to heal and take a break in between relationships. We can also move away from prayer when we are angry at what has happened, The truth is, we sometimes fell drained and do not feel like doing anything. Anger can have you thinking the Father has forgotten about you. Prayer becomes the last thing you want to do when you feel like He has failed you. I can recall countless times where I blamed God for what happened in my life. When my mom passed from Congestive Heart Failure, my faith was shaken to the core. I was at my prime of praising and worshipping God. I was on the right path, and nothing was stopping my progress. When she passed, anger hit me hard. I no longer wanted to pray because I blamed Him for allowing my mom to pass. She was the sweetest woman I had ever known. She helps so many without a single complaint. She also loves the Lord. She treated others with respect, even the ones I didn't think deserved it. She was the prime example of a woman of prayer and virtue. People around her gave her respect and gleaned from her wisdom. She had an amazing reputation. Many would refer to her as Momma.

I remember telling God that it was not fair and that I needed more time with her. I questioned why she deserved to die before she could experience me taking care of her. I remember it just like it was on yesterday. With my face full of tears, I looked upward and said those words. I was so angry. In my moment of anger, I heard a still, small voice say, "She asked me to come home." I was not ready for that response. However, even in the anger, hurt, pain, and disappointment, I had to make my way back to prayer. My anger pushed me right back to prayer. Praying is a cause to get an understanding. With all thy getting, get an understanding is what the Word says. Even in my questioning and His response, God showed He loved me unconditionally. He could have turned a deaf ear and kept silent. Instead, He took me down memory lane of the many conversations my mom and I held before she passed. The day before she passed, she mentioned to me how excited she was. She let me know that the Lord had shown her so much while being in the hospital. Her excitement was as if she had been given good news concerning her healing. I didn't know that she had gotten a glimpse of heaven and was ready to leave. In my selfishness, I wanted her to be here forever. God honored her prayer of living to see her daughters grow into women. Later on, I realized that she had a conversation with my aunt about leaving without saying. One of the things mentioned was how she thought all of her daughter were in good places of life. She went on to voice her concern of me seeing how I worry the most. Even as a child, my fear was always of her passing away while I was still young. You can never fully be prepared for death. I'm so glad that in my anger, the Lord demonstrated giving me the truth and understanding. The truth was able to free me from being angry. He who the son has set free is free indeed. Although I lacked understanding, the Lord's love met me where I was. This gave me the vigor to increase my prayer life. I knew the Lord would not steer me wrong. That gave me such a peace and comfort to know my mom would not be suffering any longer. Although I miss her immensely, I have peace that passes all understanding over my heart and mind. The blessing is that she still lives through my sisters and I. I look so much like her that it is scary at times. She would tell me all the time how much I remind her of herself. From my style, to my heart for people and many other things. I cherish those moments and memories and use it as inspiration plus motivation. She was certainly a woman who was sure in who she was in Christ. To know that she had a relationship with the

Lord and watching her serve helped me not to make excuses.

Just because you're a woman of prayer, it does not exempt you from having feelings or emotions. I believe sometimes because of who we are in Christ, it applies pressure. It causes to fear feeling and influences us to respond differently. We must not forget that we are human. We will feel! Sometimes we can do that due to our own perceptions of how we think. We should respond as a believer. There are times when others try to dictate how you respond to grief or to life emotionally.

I pray that this helps someone who is struggling. I pray that it causes you to plug in or plug back in to the source. We hear so many things about what we shouldn't do when it comes to praying and our walk. We have been told not to question God. I beg to differ. Again, the Word tells us to get understanding. It builds wisdom. I wasn't wrong in asking the Lord about my mom. He answered so that I could walk in freedom and not in discouragement, pain or anger from grief. Let your journey be your journey! Ask as many questions as you'd like to the Lord. This is how relationships work. When we don't know, we ask to gain clarity and understanding. It will keep you connected to the source which is Christ. A prime example I can remember is when I was getting ready to worship before cleaning. I was attempting to connect my phone to my Bluetooth speaker. I sat for about 4-5 minutes trying to figure out why it wouldn't connect. I finally realized that the Bluetooth speaker wasn't plugged in. I heard the Holy Spirit in that moment. Stay connected to the Source! In order to ger the music to play, it has to be connected to the source. The socket receives the power needed to supply the Bluetooth. When you are connected to the source, you have power. With His power, we have strength. Throughout the Word, we hear power and how it is linked to connection. I encourage you to stay connected even when you do not understand. I am thankful that in my anger, it led me right back to the source for reconnection. When people tell others not to ask God questions, I believe it can detour them or cause disconnection from the source. If I hadn't gone to the source, I may have walked away from the faith. I could have possibly not even returned to it. This is also the importance of having an intimate relationship with the Lord. This enables you to be led by the Holy Spirit.

Lord, I thank you for not turning me away like people. Thank you for answering my concerns without aggravation! I've always been an inquisitive person, so I am grateful for His patience with me as well. Some people have no tolerance for inquisitive people. They fail to realize that we ask for understanding and not from being nosey. They feel we are not intelligent or that we get on others' nerves with ignorance. I am so glad to serve a God who doesn't mind the questions. I encourage people to ask the Lord questions. Go to the Lord about your concerns as this keeps you connected to the source.

My Prayer

Father, I thank you for those who have turned away and disconnected from you out of anger, disappointment, or unanswered questions. I pray they go back to the source Lord, which is you. Even in their anger, hear them ... even in their pain, hear them....

even in their anger, hear them .. even in their shame. Father hear them. Let them know that you are always there and there isn't anything that they can't ask for. You said you will perfect that which concerns them. Lord, I thank you in this very moment of this prayer that you began to speak to them about their concerns. In Matthew 11:28, you said come to you all who are heavy laden and you will give them rest. So I thank you that they enter rest. That they cast every care on you for you care for them, I pray that the anger, pain, resentment, and fear that they've held in for years will fall suddenly. Thank you that they will boast in your goodness. I thank you for your Word to perform it. That your Word will not return void and it shall accomplish that which it set out to do. It shall prosper in the thing which you have sent it to do according to Isaiah 55:11. We declare it to be so.

In Jesus' Name.

Amen

CHAPTER 4

Preparation

Preparation is the key to getting to the promise. Being a woman of prayer will position you to prepare for what's next. Preparation is something that's needed in every area of life. We have to prepare for the next level whatever it may be. For example, we go to college to get an education. It also prepares you for that particular career field that you've studied for months. There is always something required of you while in your preparation process. Preparation is putting your faith in motion and doing your part. It's working your part of faith. Remember, faith without works is dead. When seeking employment, we put in an application or resume. To lose weight, we eat right and exercise. You get the point of the part that we must play. Sometimes, it's our lack of preparation that causes our promise to be prolonged. Preparation is doing the work even when you don't feel like it. We even have a part to play in our own healing. It's our responsibility to heal from what or who hurt us. Many of us have asked for something that we weren't ready for because we lacked preparation. Has that ever happened to you? The right blessing seems to be the wrong timing. I've heard people say that they wanted a spouse but met someone at the wrong time in their life. I've heard women say, "He was a good guy but I had so much going on at the time I couldn't give him the time of day." I have even heard that they were giving the person a hard time because of their unhealed trauma. They could have been a good person with all the qualities they had asked for, but they weren't ready.

It's such a blessing to not rush to get to the promise without preparation. Has someone ever showed up to your home and you felt like you weren't prepared? You felt the need to have to quickly get put together. Someone once said, "If you stay ready, you don't have to get ready. That statement is so true. If we prepare properly, we don't have to fear being caught off guard. I remember being in transition. I had closed my second hair salon in place of become a traveling hairstylist. In that season, I remember having more time to be at home. I found myself getting comfortable so much so that I felt like I was never prepared for anything. Even in something as simple as meeting a friend for lunch. I still had my faith outstretched for the things that were on my faith plate. The moment I realized that I had become comfortable, I realized how unprepared I was for what I was asking for. If the Lord would have allowed what was on my faith plate to manifest, I would have been all over the place. I wouldn't have known how to properly receive it. When we look at things from a place of love rather than hate, we would see that all things work together for our good. The Lord isn't keeping any good thing from us. As a matter of fact, He said that He would not withhold any good thing from those who walk upright. Again, we have to do our part to prepare and let everything else fall into place. I know it may seem easier said than done but consider asking yourself how bad do you want it?! Preparation doesn't mean that you won't be challenged. You may question how long should you prepare but that shouldn't be your focus. You can open the door of being anxious. Anxiousness may rear it's head along with fear. Be anxious for nothing for He is with you, even in preparation. He is the one preparing you. Fear will have you thinking that you are doing all this work in vain. Cast down every imagination, bring into captivity every thought and set it under the obedience of christ. We have to shut down those negative thoughts immediately. When they show up so they won't be able to fester into fear, doubt, and unbelief. One of the ways to shut this down is to think about what you're thinking about. That is wisdom from my former pastor. If we immediately examine our thoughts and speak the Word over the negative ones, we would probably realize it's necessary. Your thoughts can take you down a rabbit hole and will have you confused as to how you got there. One of the things I've learned dealing with anxiety is that you have to immediately arrest negative thoughts. Speak the truth, which is the Word, to yourself. Speak it out loud so that those thoughts have no place To give those thoughts no place.

Anxiety is the simply the spirit of fear. He hasn't given you the spirit of fear but of love, power and a sound mind. I realized that fear is always anticipating something bad to happen. Faith is the opposite. It's anticipating something good to happen. Fear and faith can't co-exist. You either have one or the other. I learned how anxiety played a major part in some of my life decisions as well as in my preparation process. I had to do some things scared. I declared the Word, 2 Timothy 1:7, over my life while preparing for what was next. I refused to allow a Spirit that the Lord didn't give me, to consume or hinder me from the promises of God. Fear is torment but perfect love cast's it out. (1 John 4:18). I began to operate in this scripture on purpose. It blessed my life tremendously.

I challenge you to pray and ask the Lord what are the areas you should be preparing in so that you're not all over the place. It can be as simple as going to bed on time because your next level or promise will require another level of rest and strength. Make sure you're not dismissive to the instructions given because they are considered simple. Simple is always valid when you're instructed. If I can encourage you, move as instructed. Everyone won't understand your journey. It's not for them to understand. When I began to prepare for next level of life. I was so used to working for myself. Making my own schedule had me a little spoiled. What I didn't realize is what my next season required. Old habits had to be broken. My next level was more structured and more routine. It was a challenge for me because for 20-plus years, I had been going to bed at different times (depending on my schedule). This is also why I encourage you to keep your ear to the Father's mouth. Hear and be obedient. I was prompted a year or so prior to my life shift. I ignored that prompt thinking I had time. I dismissed what seemed to be minor instructions. It was so vital for the next season. It required me to be up hours before I was used to getting up, lifting, and traveling. Obedience is better than sacrifice. Your obedience is needed in the process. The moment I got in position, the next level to my promise flowed with ease. The

Lord really wants us to succeed. It's a matter of tuning in to get daily instruction and following suit with the instructions. I can't tell you how many times I was disobedient, asking God what to do next when I hadn't followed through with the first set of instructions. Sometimes we are our own hold up. We are crying out asking the Lord to prepare us. We are asking Him what to do and haven't done what He said in 2014.

One of the reasons to why some may say the Lord isn't saying anything while in prayer, is because of that very reason. You may feel like you have been praying over and over. Perhaps, you may need to go back and ask Him to bring back to your remembrance if any instructions were given that you missed or forgot about. I have had to do this several times. I always do it, even if I think I followed suit with instructions. I rather be sure than to repeat the season or prolong my next level and promise. Remember, obedience is better than sacrifice. I want to hear and obey. Let's be prepared. Just think about that the next time you pray. Ask yourself:

"Am I prepared?"

"Have I followed suit with the instructions given"

"Have I been obedient and consistent with the instructions?"

"Have I let the instructions slip?"

One thing we can't do is, do only part of the instructions and then expect God to do His part. We have to do our part not a part. That's why it's good to ask even if you think you've crossed all your T's and doted all of your I's. So, when you petition the Lord about your promise and know that you've done your part, you can stand in full anticipation with confidence. He honors obedience. Parents you know that it makes you proud when your children listen and do the things you've asked. The same for our Heavenly Father. He loves when we hear and heed His instructions. I look back at how many situations I could have avoided if I would have listened. I have ears to hear so I choose to hear. I have eyes to see so I choose to see. I don't want to hear and not listen or see and disregard what is shown to me. The Word says that His sheep knows His voice, the voice of a stranger they will not follow.

Going back to ask the Lord about your instructions, if you missed it or forgot, will also help you not to blame God or people. It keeps you from having a victim's mentality. You will soon realize the part you've played in your own story. This is not a moment to beat yourself up when He does take you back to what you've missed. There is no condemnation for those that are in Christ. I encourage you to have hope. This is your moment to get back on track and prepare for what's coming. We all have missed a moment. What I realized is that I don't want to repeat the same season over if I don't have to. I want to be aware in that moment to make the adjustment rather than to repeat it. If i can be brutally honest, I remember the Lord sending little reminders. He sent little reminders to get me back on track through people and situations. That's His love and His way of showing how much He desired for me to get back on the path of preparation. His love just blows my mind. When we sing : "When I think of His goodness and all that He has done for me", my soul cries out, Hallelujah! If you just go down memory lane for a few minutes, you will surely be grateful. That will keep you focused on the part you play in your own story. You will be reminded how good He has been … even when we didn't deserve it. He's faithful just like that! His love for us is unconditional if we only open our hearts to it. We will know that He really wants His best for us. I'm so thankful that you are not like man. You don't just throw us away at a mere mistake or when we miss the mark. Lord, I thank you for your loving kindness and your tender mercies. Lord, you are good and you are God alone. I give you glory honor and praise!

Declare this with me:

> *Lord, I arrest condemnation right now in the name of Jesus. I will not let condemnation take root. Before I ask you to bring back to my remembrance what I missed or forgot by way of instructions, Lord, I thank you for your love. I thank you that you love me so much that you will even give me the instructions all over again. Lord, you are awesome! Go before me as I prepare for what I am asking for. I thank you that I am not anxious for anything. Help me to be content in the state that I'm in as you prepare me for my next and for my promise. Help me to keep my eyes on you*

Lord. Lord, give me the strength mentally, physically, emotionally as I go forth with your instructions. Lord, I thank you for keeping me focused, even when distractions show up. I thank you for the thoughts and plans you have for me. Plans to prosper me and not harm me, plans to give me hope and a future. I thank you Lord, that I trust you to prepare the way you see fit in how to prepare me. I take my plan off the table God. I submit to your plan because you know what's best for me. Lord, help me to see immediately when I seem to veer off your plan so that I may quickly get back on track. Lord, I thank you that I'm careful for nothing; but in everything by prayer and supplication with thanksgiving. I make my request known to you Lord. I thank you that the peace that passes all understanding will keep my heart and mind.

In Jesus' Name

Amen!

I tell you today my friend, prepare now! Let this be your reminder to prepare for what is next and for what you are asking God for. Do the work (whatever that looks like). Keep your ear to the Lord's mouth to get daily instructions and prepare for what is next. Everyone's instructions will be different. Don't compare your preparation season to anyone else's. Just make sure you hear and heed your instructions. You're responsible for what you have to do, not others.

CHAPTER 5

The Detox

We promote detoxing our bodies through proper diet, detox pills, teas, juices, etc, but often we don't hear about detoxing from or between relationships. When we take a detox for our body, once it's time to release, no one goes to the restroom with us. It's just you. The purpose of that detox is for your health and well-being. I'm simply saying that it's necessary to detox in between relationships. It's for your benefit, which means no one can do the work for you. That doesn't mean you can't have people in your corner cheering you on. The detox will rid you of hurt, shame, unforgiveness, anger, resentment, and the list goes on. When you work on yourself, you set yourself up to become a better version of yourself. It'll also add value to others life.

A LADY IN WAITING

Have you ever met someone and all they talked about was their Ex?! Oh, what a turnoff! Either they haven't healed or they're not over them. When we are healed, the only way an Ex comes up is, if the conversation goes in that direction. No one volunteers past info, especially if you've met a potential new love. The last thing you want to talk about is your past. This is why some people go from person to person. All they are doing is meeting the same person, just in a different body. We don't like it done to us, right?! Just imagine doing that to someone when you're not healed. The detox was the best decision I could've ever made. It made me choose me. The detox means choosing you.

I'm a giver by nature. Givers have to be mindful because we can attract takers. People take in different ways. The way that some would try to take from me was taking my sweetness for weakness. One would assume that because I'm gentle, feminine, easy-going and easy to forgive, I'm easy to get over on. During my detox process. I had a chance to deal with myself. To look deeply into my actions, responses, and what

I allowed, I realized that some of my actions needed to be evaluated. I needed to get to the root of where my issues and actions originated from. I had to ask myself: " Why are you too nice?!", "Why do you need to stay longer than you should in relationships?!" Most people who are too nice lack boundaries, and we have a hard time saying no. People deem that as a push over. I learned how to set boundaries. I learned to let my No's be No and my Yes's be Yes. During that process, I also learned that I was a people pleaser. I tried to please everyone, even at the expense of my happiness. I remember that at the beginning of my cosmetology career, I had a large clientele. Although I had a large clientele. I would still take referrals because I loved what I do. Among the referrals, it allowed me to take on new clients. I worked for years straight, taking no vacations or days off. Some customers would reschedule or cancel for various reasons. Which was understandable. I remember squeezing people in at any given time. Although that worked for me in that season, I should've set boundaries. Years later, when things began to shift for me, I started setting boundaries. Some became offended because I would no longer accommodate what worked best for them. One customer went as far as to message me. She stated how she was perplexed because I couldn't squeeze her in last minute for her birthday. She went on to say that she was with me for 9 plus years even when my prices were inconsistent. The crazy part is, her view of me changed in that single moment, even though I serviced her for 9 years. This included not taking any days off, never being late, and always making accommodations. It opened my eyes seeing how people responded to my boundaries, which further solidified setting them. Through her cancellations and late arrivals. To being helpful by only charging her between $25-$35 depending on what services were rendered, never exceeding $35. She was really offended by my boundaries. Takers don't mind taking. I became okay with losing clients to gain those who would respect my business and boundaries. Some were used to the old version of me that had none. The moment I set those boundaries, some felt entitled! What was in their heart came out. Moral of the story: I learned boundaries at the expense of losing. I learned so much about myself during the process of detoxing. Your taste buds change when you're healed versus when you're not. Some people's journeys may be different. Some may require counseling, meditating on the word of God, or the company of good friends or people. Sometimes, it takes all of the above. I chose to meditate on the Word. I found my situation in the Word. Through the Word, I gained mental clarity as well as learned my worth. I'm able to view things with a clear mental instead of being led by my emotions. When we are hurt or emotionally wounded, we become emotionally led instead of spirit-led. Your emotions will have you making decisions based on how you feel rather than being led by the Holy Spirit. How many times have we not felt like going to work, cleaning up, or picking up the kids? The truth is we may not feel like it but, it has to be done. If you did what you felt most of the time, we wouldn't get most things done. So, we can't live on feelings. I learned not to allow feeling to move me into ignoring the truth. I searched what the Word of God said about me. Your feelings will lie to you. It'll tell you things that go contrary to what the Word of God says about you. I began to speak the Word daily over my life. I no longer answered to the old version of me. Whether it were through people or my emotions, I chose not to answer. There's a saying that says: "We teach people how to treat us." This is so true. I would rather be respected than liked. I wrote my plan down as to how I wanted to run my business and the way I wanted to be treated in both, my business and personal life. Anything that no longer served me peace or purpose, I either cut it off or adjusted it to the new boundaries and way of life.

A habit I had was always coming to other's rescue instead of allowing people to figure things out. I also wasn't using wisdom concerning who to help. I don't know if I would have gotten to the root of the problem if I hadn't detoxed. I probably wouldn't have known the extent of my problems. I would not have been able to establish how to set healthy boundaries. Of course, not setting boundaries in business were a mere reflection of other areas in my life. Those areas included allowing myself to stay too long in relationships, friendships, or business-ships.

Some people didn't deserve front row seats and access to my life. Now, the healed version of me has a no-tolerance policy, in those areas. Detoxing taught me to take responsibility for being too nice. There is nothing wrong with loving christ, being a believer, or being kind. Another area for me was emotions. Because I am an empath, I felt everything. I had to learn not to allow my feelings to move me. Remember being emotionally led can cause you to move in a way that contradicts the Word as well as what you hear the Holy Spirit tell you to do. People will play on your ability to always understand and empathize with them. I stayed in my detox season until certain boundaries were completely set in stone. I use that season of my life to practice telling people no … without wavering. I had to learn that people will talk regardless of what you choose to do. My former pastor would often say: "If you would like to go further in what you are called to do, you can't worry about the opinions of other's".. I can look back at how many times God gave me vision for my life. It was many people who didn't necessarily believe the vision God gave me. It was ok because it wasn't for them to believe the vision. The Lord gave it to me not them.

Just like detoxing our bodies has its benefits, so does detoxing from previous relationships. Everyone will gain something different but it's for your good. Have you ever met someone in between relationships? Some call it a rebound. For the moment, it seems to be what you wanted. However, when you begin to take your focus off of the hurt, you realize you don't even like the person! It makes you want to say to people who do love you: "Why in the world did you let me entertain that person?" I can raise my hand on that. Most of the time, your method of choosing comes from brokenness. Whatever you carry, you will attract. A man can point out when a woman is performing from emotions. Some intentionally seek that out and become what you want to get to whatever he's after. You're more susceptible and open emotionally to accept the shenanigans because you're wounded and not healed. The healed you will see right through the pretenses. Just like some men can see the hurt, some men can see the healed version of you.

They will be less likely to play games. Even if he does, you're able to discern quickly. One you've spent time in the Word, you will be built up mentally, emotionally, and spiritually. Your discernment will be heightened and you will begin to view relationships differently. You will not play about you." You understand what it took to get you to where you are in all areas. You take your power back when you detox. I believe when you have not properly healed or tamed your emotions, people have open opportunity to distract you from properly healing. Some men will present themselves as an angel of light to make you think; " Oh this is my knight in shining armor. Heal first so you can determine if it is a decoy or an imposter. Let's be honest … it wouldn't be fair for a man to show up in our lives and experience the wrath of what some else has done to us. As women, we wouldn't want that done to us so we should consider the man as well. A refusal to heal will have you taking them through hell and back. That is something that is undeserved. Let's heal together. Nothing is more powerful than a woman being honest with herself as to where she is mentally, emotionally, spiritually, and physically. Healing properly and allowing yourself to heal through detoxing is necessary. Detoxing will have you showing up powerful, healed and whole. It will give you clarity, confidence, and peace. You got this!

CHAPTER 6

Timing

Timing is everything. The Lord's timing will prevent detours and roadblocks. In a previous chapter, I spoke on how some things have shown up in our lives out of being unprepared. The Lord's timing for our life is perfect. He knows when we are mature enough to handle what we are asking for. Time can be waiting on you to mature as well. Maybe you lack wisdom. He gives you the opportunity to get wisdom because His timing is necessary. What is for you will not pass you by. In Psalm 34:10 it states: *Those who seek God, shall lack no good thing.* In Isaiah 60:22 it tells us that the Lord will quicken it in its own time. The Lord will make it happen. Every season we are in or the things that we go through is in the Word. If you're in the season of His timing, go to the Word of God concerning it.

Find scriptures to pray while you wait. Put the Lord in remembrance of His Word who is faithful to perform it. The Lord knows what's ahead. There is an appointed time for everything and there is a time for every event under Heaven (Ecclesiastes 3:1). The Lord's timing is an appointed time frame or duration He has set for something to unfold. His time is different from ours. The fact that we don't know when our promises will come to pass can led to worry, doubt, fear and unbelief. We can all be a little impatient at times. No one is exempt as it's a natural response. Many mistakes can be avoided if we truly trust Him and flow with His timing. We get to enjoy the beauty of His promises if we would only wait on Him. Everything the Lord promises, is beautiful. Learn to celebrate the beauty in waiting. The way you view things can either help or hinder you. Change your mind and you can change your life. Remember that as a man thinks in his heart, so is he. Think on the things that are true, pure, good (Philippians 4:8-9). Think on these things. If you view His timing negatively, you will have what you think. Timing and process is a part of the plan. Think about that for a moment?! Timing takes a lot of patience and strength.

However, He will reward our patience if we stay the course. It will be worth the wait. Oftentimes, we can miss out on God's timing out of our impatient nature. Rushing God's timing speaks as if we know better than Him. We must realize that He planned our end from the beginning. Time is on our side when we're waiting on His will to be done. We have to be intentional with staying on the path.

Biological clocks is another thing that can push us out of His will. It will have you worrying unnecessarily. It can have you worrying when will you be married, wanting to remarry without wisdom, fearing that you're too old to wait, worrying about having children, or even worrying about buying a house. To add to that, social media seems to have us think that we have front row seats into other people's lives. We start considering goals that mirror those same people we do not know. personally. That's their story, not yours. Looking at the lives of other people can get you out of the will. We can be so interested and invested into other peoples lives that we miss out on our own timing. We miss out on the promises from God. His timing will require your patience and strength along with your focus. Staying focused while waiting on God's timing has it's challenges, just like any other season. His timing should be a big deal to you, especially, if you've tried to do thing's your way and it didn't work out. It's time to get back in His will. I've learned that you have to have a made-up mind. No one can force you. The Lord himself doesn't even force His will on us. He gives us free will to do whatever we want; however, we have to live with the decisions we make.

I take his timing very seriously. The way I see it is that I have come to far to turn back. Imagine working hard to accomplish a goal and right before you accomplish that goal, you do something without thinking that results in forfeiting that goal. All the hard work would be a disservice to you. Going in knowing that it would forfeit that goal that you've work so hard to accomplish, would you do it? I'm guessing your response would be no. The is the way I view my choices before I allow my emotions to take me off the path. Recognizing that those impulsive decisions out of God's timing can cause me to not only forfeit my goal, but the prospect of having to start over too. Having to start completely over can be discouraging at times. I don't want to waste any more time. I've seen when I've taken matters into my own hands. I've seen where thinking I knew what worked best for me, landed me. It landed me in relationships and places I could have avoided. We should all get to a place where we are sick and tired of our own shenanigans. You're not tired until you're sick and tired. Get out of your own way so that things can flourish in your life. The season's come with maturity. (Notice I didn't say age). It takes maturity to recognize that you've gotten out of the Lord's will and His timing. It also takes maturity not to blame anything or anyone. You notice it and you take the necessary steps to get back on track. Remember, how bad do you want it?!

I remember moving in with this young lady right after the passing of my mom. This young lady had asked me to be her roommate. This became one of the biggest mistakes I've ever made. I didn't ask the Lord, I just did it. I thought because we had so much in common that it would be easy. We were a part of the same ministry and both single with no children. I thought it would be a good fit. I knew I was suppose to move, I just didn't realize it wasn't supposed to have been with her. It also was not the right timing. That was a nightmare from hell. Prior to my mom's passing, she told me what she observed concerning that young lady. My mother had warned me about her. She was controlling and jealous of my influence. In that moment, I realized that people can have more and still be jealous. That's just the surface of what I experienced living there. The very things my mom saw years prior is what I experienced. I'll put a period right there as the Lord knows that one is for another book. I am thankful, I was in my twenties at the time. To think back to that moment makes me even more grateful! I'm so glad that I learned so much. I gained at lot of wisdom. Needless to say, I had to start over since I moved in my own timing instead of His. That experience birthed another level of gratefulness. It taught me a valuable lesson which was not to follow my own path.

Seek first his kingdom, his way of doing things and everything else will be provided for me (Mathew 6:33).

I trust His timing, even when I don't fully understand what He's doing. I rest in what Jerimiah 29:11 tells me. The process seemed a little harder after getting off track. I knew better. When we know better, we should do better. It can cost us if we're not mindful. This is why I express the importance of waiting on His timing. Another area that can get us out of God's timing is adding and subtracting from the Word of God. When we do that, we can become wise in our own mind's thinking that we are right. For instance, you hear the Lord tell you while in you're waiting that He's doing a new thing, but that's all you heard. Now you're trying to finish His sentence by adding or subtracting from what you heard. You begin trying to interpret that

Word to co-sign on an unwise decision you know you're about to make. When I hear a Word spoken, I ask for clarity so I won't move on what I think the Lord is saying. Trust that even while waiting, He will reveal what He's saying to you. If we aren't careful of doing this we can open the door to offense. This is how offense comes in and becomes a stumbling block. It'll try and stop you from getting back on track.

I urge you to get back on track. Ask for understanding the next time the Lord speaks. I share my experiences in hope to prevent someone from making the same choices I did. If you happen to be in the midst of being out of His timing, let me help you get back on track. Take the information and move on what the Lord is inclining you to do. Whether that is getting back on track or staying on track. et this be your inspiration. I recognize that we all think differently as well as have different experiences. The one thing I've learned is that I'd rather learn from other's mistakes than have to learn through experience. I've heard experience is the best teacher. I slightly disagree. Some things can be prevented with the wisdom from someone who has gone down that path. We have to take to take heed when wisdom is poured into our lives. This is especially when we are blessed to have people in our lives that pour into us. Don't take that for granted.

Repeat after me:

> *Lord, I recognize that I got out of your timing by being impatient. By trying to do thing's in my own strength, I wasn't fruitful. Lord, I repent for getting off course. Lord, I recommit to the process of waiting on your timing. You know the when and how it will all come to pass, because you knew me before I was formed in my mother's womb. I thank you for being a pattient God.. one that is patient with me. Help me when I am anxious, fearful, or in doubt about your timing. Remind me that your timing is perfect. You are the source of my strength. I thank you for your strength as I wait. Help me to keep my eye's on you while I wait for your timing. Lord, keep me steadfast, unmoveable, and always abounding in your work. Help me to not become weary in well doing sothat I may reap for fainting not (Galatian 6:9). Ipray for focus, strength, peace and patience for your timing. I wanna trust you*

Lord in this process. I need help with that Lord. I thank you for this prayer. I believe and recieve all that I've prayed. I thank you and praise you.

In Jesus' Name

Amen.

CHAPTER 7

Promise

Waiting on the promise can have you doubting everything! Your emotions will try to have a field day with you. I've thrown adult temper tantrums because things didn't happen when I thought they should. Scripture tell us: "He knows the thoughts and plans that He has for us, that are good and not for evil, to give us an expected end". (Jeremiah 29:11) He's a God of timing. His timing is perfect. Nobody desires to wait, especially living in a microwaveable society. Whatever people want in this day and time, can now be given in an instant. This microwave society says I want it all and I want it now. Truth is, that is not reality. The process is different for everyone. Some people process seems to take longer than others. We've seen this demonstrated throughout the Word of God as well as in life. I really became intentional with learning and understanding my process. Learning what waiting looked like for me and how I could do my part with grace. With waiting comes emotions. You can find yourself angry, frustrated, complaining, and the list can goes on. In order to be intentional while waiting on my promise, I had to surrender the timeframe I had in mind. Let's talk about that for a few minutes. One of the ways that'll add or cause disappointment is writing out your own timeline as to how things should play out in your life. You will come to realize, the Lord, has planned your end from the beginning. I began to truly surrender my promises to the Lord. What did that look like for me? It meant praying with intentionality, surrendering, and receiving the continual grace of waiting.

My Prayer

Lord, I thank for the Word you gave me concerning your promise. Lord, you said that you know the thoughts and plans that you have for me. That are good to give me an expected end. I expect the end to this promise you're giving me. Lord, you said that your promises are yes and amen. Thefore, I take you at your Word for you are faithful to perform it. You said that your Word will not return to you void and will do in which it was sent out to do. Thefore Lord, I surrender all. My will, my plans, my time frame, and my ideas. Your will be done. Help me to rest knowing if you said it, it is so. I decrease so that you increase Lord. I'm done with trying things on my own, in my own strength. I'm burnt out. Here I am lord. Thank you for your grace as I wait on your promises for my life. I thank you, Lord and I ask for strength mentally, physically, spiritually, and emotionally. Lord, I ask you to surround me with the right people at this time. Protect my heart, my ear and eye gate so that I may stay focused. Lord, help me to remain focused as distractions come.

In Jesus' Name,

Amen.

In my prayer, I make sure I acknowledge and surrender my ways, put the Lord in remembrance of his Word, and then ask for what I need to help me on the journey. I make sure to be consistent with my prayers until I see my promise come to pass. Though it tarry it will come to pass. Remember, His promises are yes and amen. How challenging that season of my life was. I know I heard the Lord and He confirmed His word multiple times. I still have to walk it out. I talk about this moment in life with such transparency because I believe in sharing the complete truth. It's not easy but God! To have things going on in your life while simultaneously believing and waiting on the promise takes a certain type of strength. That strength comes from the Lord. I remember hearing the other day that it'll be worth the wait. Now, that word from the Lord encouraged me on a whole other level. One thing I can say is that the Lord will give little reminders to encourage you on the way to the promise. This is to keep you encouraged. It's moments like those that give you the help you need to keep going … despite how you feel. Remember, feelings are temporary. Although I acknowledge and validate them, I'm aware that feelings easily change. My prayer concerning my emotions is: "Lord, sit on the throne of my emotions. Help me to be led by your spirit and not my emotions".

In your emotions dwells no good thing. As women, we have to be aware of our emotions and triggers. I know for me, when it's closer to that time of month, I cry just because. I already wear my heart on my sleeve so during that time, I ask the Father to make me aware of the time. The truth is, we can get so busy with life that we may not be aware in that moment. That's why I ask the Lord to make me aware of my emotions. When I become aware, I declare the joy of the Lord is my strength. I believe we need strength in every season and situation. It is most certainly needed when waiting on your promise. I also drench myself in worship. The other day, I heard a clip of a worship song that said: "Lord, have your way in me". The song was titled, I Surrender, by Matt Crocker and Hillsong. The chorus was simple testimony of what my prayer had been. Remember, I said the Lord will send little reminders to encourage you along the way. That's my way of knowing that He will not only perfect what concerns me, but He will also remind me that He hears me when I pray. The Lord is so awesome! I just thank him for keeping me on this journey .I thank Him for also being a keeper on my celibacy journey. When you want more, you do more. When we want to lose a few pounds, we do what we need to, to get it done. Same thing applies to Christ. How bad do we want the promise?. I'm sharing my journey to help, but as for me and my house?! … you know the rest. His promise to me is allowing me to have my person to do life with. When you have several failed relationships, it can cause you to feel like a failure. I am a gentle, feminine, and classy woman. I have absolutely no desire to operate in any level of masculinity. I desire to be properly led through submission. I don't mind submitting to the correct leadership. Let me clarify. I want to be led by a man who is truly after God's heart, has a purpose-driven life, that understands purpose and how to stay focused. One that complements what's on my life vice versa. That doesn't mean rulership, being controlled or not having a voice. That's just a short version of what I mean by submitting. Submission is not bad at all. Submission is an attitude. The mission gives you a place to sub alongside of. It's willingly coming under the authority of another. I will sub under the mission I'm called to with my man of

God. I'm okay with that. Let my moments be motivation for you to stay encouraged. I am walking this promise out as I write (July 2024). Hold fast to the promise given. It shall come to pass. Father, I thank you for every person who is believing for their promise.

My Prayer

Lord, I ask that you give them patience, grace to wait, and peace in knowing that your Word will not return void. It will do that in which it was sent out to do. That your promises are yes and amen. If you said it, it is so. Give them the peace that passes all understanding. Give them peace over their heart and mind. Let them rest in you. Lord, I ask that you send them little reminders as they wait to keep them encouraged.

In Jesus' Name,

Amen.

CHAPTER 8
Worth The Wait

Waiting pays off, contrary to popular belief. I know many won't see wating as worth it, but it is. I remember coming across this picture of Jesus and a little girl. The little girl was holding a small teddy bear. The picture depicted Jesus holding a much bigger teddy bear behind His back to give to her. All she needed to do was give Him the one she had. That picture spoke volumes. Many times, we don't want to give up what we have for better. Anytime the Lord asks you to give up something, He always has something better. I believe when we know our worth, we won't settle for less. If we can get to a place where anything that show's up in our lives that isn't a God promise, we dont allow it in, we would be so much better. Knowing your worth can take time but we have to stop accepting anything less than the Lord's best for us. Most people settle for what they think they deserve. Please know that you are worthy of God's best.

Some of us have been settling our whole lives because of the lies that were told to us as a children or due to environment. I use to hear people speak on how opposites attract. Just hearing that, my assumptions were based off what people would share about concerning the love journey. I assumed that physical wasn't something important or you shouldn't necessarily take it into consideration. I would hear how some would say that their person, initially, wasn't their type physically. I understood their viewpoint. They were sharing to help other's to not be shallow when choosing a spouse, However, I believe there is nothing wrong with wanting physical attraction as well. Your "why" of not choosing someone you're physically attracted to, shouldn't be based off settling. The crazy part is, I would see this mostly in church settings. I wasn't raised that way. I soon realized that was their journey. I believe you should get what you want which is His promises for your life. I have to give balance to this. It's so easy to interpret things to fit what you think you want but it's not a part of His Will for your life. I say get what you know the Lord promised you. Don't settle for nothing less than what He promised. He said He will bless you with the desires of your heart if you delight yourself in him. (Psalm 37:4).

Some of the instructions that were given to prepare me for my promises, challenged me to get rid of everything old. From clothes, shoes, pictures, and even furniture, I started getting rid of it. I even disconnected from people. I wanted to follow all the instructions given. I was over trying to do things on my own. I got tired of starting over because I wanted to do things my way. I was tired of my own shenanigans. We can so easily get tired of other people's ways instead of our own. When you're truly ready for change, you won't easily allow things to get in the way. I'll keep saying it. How bad do you want it?! I love to say we play a part in our own story. We can either add to it through obedience or subtract by being disobedient. The moment I stayed in position of obedience, my promises were a domino effect. When the Lord told me He would give me a salon, it was a challenge yet it was worth it. The Lord gave me this Word right after being asked to leave a salon I was working at. The owner rented a booth out to me during a difficult season. As she interviewed me, she began to speak death over my business. She stated that because I was new to the business, I would not have clients and expect it not to work out for me. She went on and on about how it wouldn't work out. Not even a week later, I had so many clients that they couldn't fit in the lobby. The more my clientele grew, the more jealousy reared it's ugly head. My clientele had always been very professional, stylish and down to earth. The owner would make comments to my customers out of spite just to get a reaction out of me. She was old enough to be my mom so I was appalled by her action towards my customers and I. What I realized is that what she spoke over me didn't come from a genuine place. She was offended because what she spoke over me didn't manifest. What she spoke over me is what happened to her business. He prepared a table before me in the presence my enemy (Psalm 23:5). She had to watch me everyday and be reminded of the blessings and favor on my life. We have to be careful who we put our mouth on. I worked there for a few months until the owner asked me to leave the salon. She did this right in front of my client's. I was furious because I knew it was the spirit of jealousy. Despite me paying rent on time, even before time on some occasions, she asked me to leave. I still loved on her even when she seem loveable. I remember hearing the Holy Spirit say to me: "Shake her hand and thank her for the opportunity". I did just that. In the midst of me packing up, the Lord said: "Double for your trouble and shame. Persue ownership". I heard the Lord clearly. In my search and worry about where I would go, I ended up searching in the area. I was led to the salon not too far from where I already was. I walked into this salon and was very transparent with the owner. I did not tell her what had happened in full detail but I was honest about needing a booth right in that moment. She was little taken back at how adamant I was about needing a booth immediately. I walked in so much favor that day, it was unbelievable. The owner of that salon told me that I didn't have to pay her right away. She proceeded to tell me that it was something about me. She went on to tell me that this would be my salon one day. I was in awe of how the Lord immediately confirmed His Word to me. I also believe the Lord was letting me know that I was in the right place at the right time. I stayed the course despite any and everything that had happened or was happening around me. In the end, it became my salon. I worked with the owner for about a year until she came to me to let me know that she was moving to a new location. She told me that I could go with her if I wanted to. I told her I would stay because the Lord brought back to my remembrance His Word. That the salon was meant to be mine. The Lord is so good. I didn't have the money to open and get furniture at the same time. The previous owner asked me to buy her out which meant purchasing everything in the salon. I told her to let me pray it. If that was the route the Lord wanted me to take, then He would provide. I remember getting back to the owner to tell her no. She was very upset because I didn't. She became nice nasty and divulged that it was the route she had taken with the owner before her. She didn't understand my journey. That was fine because it wasn't for her to understand. I had a dream maybe a day or so after that of me walking up a staircase that wasn't there. When I would put one foot forward a step would appear until I reached the top. The Lord made it clear that faith is unseen. I trusted Him even when I couldn't trace Him. I knew that He would provide. He did just that. I experienced the "Good measure, pressed down, shaken together and running over with men pouring into my bosom". When the owner were moving out, she pretty much cleared everything. She made it clear to me that she was offended for two reasons. One that I didn't go with her (although the Lord gave her a Word for me). Two, I declined to buy her out. I knew I was faithful and served her well. She was so busy being mean that she and her moving crew could not remove the last shampoo bowl from the wall. Absolutely nothing the guy's used could remove the bowl. The men tried several times and it just wouldn't budge. It left me a shampoo bowl to start with! When you are good to people and do what's right, wish them well and keep on moving. He will fight for you

(Exodus 14:14). He'll prepare a table for you in the presence of your enemies. They have to sit and watch how they spread the table. There is absolutely nothing they can do about it! From that moment on, so many people started to sow into me. One woman asked me how much did I need for my dryers. My former pastor would always say if I didn't have the money, believe for favor. He always stressed that if the Lord sends someone to bless you with the money you need, you should always know the amount needed. Immediately, I said $500 dollars. I was blessed with a few dryers while others sowed money, purchased furniture, or paid the bills of the salon until I got settled in. I was ecstatic and in awe of His promises. I had so many clients that I had to start to turning them down. My life had changed tremendously. People who had counted me out wanted to sit in my chair to be serviced. When I tell you it is worth the wait, it is worth the wait. The flood gates had opened. I was even blessed with the type of clientele that would take care of me. They bought me expensive handbags, lunch, and paid for trips for me to go on. One of my clients paid my personal bills up for two months to give me time focus on my business. God is so awesome! Sometimes we have to be reminded that if He did it before, He will do it again. He's the same God. We forget that He a big God when in the midst of a storm or of being challenged. When we see it as worth the wait, you will be motivated to stay the course. Some of you maybe in the most difficult season of your life. It may feel like the Lord isn't with you. He is always with you; His rod and His staff will comfort you. If you don't hear anything thing else, stay the course! Many thought I wasn't ready, was too young, and that I didn't know business. The good thing about the Lord is He will direct your path while making you look good.

My hit has always been encountering the spirit of jealousy. No matter how humble, loving, supportive, or caring I would be, when it was my turn, jealousy would be present. The wisdom is to be wise in your sharing what the Lord tells you and also what He's doing. The people around me couldn't handle my success. No matter how happy and excited I was for them, it was few people that could handle when it was my turn, I realized there were two moments I would share prematurely and with the wrong people. When I would be super excited or when I would be at a low point. I'm naturally transparent so even in that, I worked against me. You could be entertaining enemies unaware. Keep your mouth closed as thing's are unfolding for you. Move in silence until what the Lord has promised ,manifests. I have countless memories of times of me opening up my mouth because I was so excited to tell the world what the Lord was doing. It was a hard pill to swallow trying to wrap my brain around why people were not happy for me when I'm always happy for them. I had to also realize that people want you to do good, just not better than them. The way that anyone feels about you is none of your business. The truth is, it's not your job to spend unecessary time and energy on that. We heard the saying, when they show you who they are, believe them. It's really for your good and you realize none of that matter's in the end. What the Lord promises is so. If i would have allowed the opinions of people to talk me out believing it's worth the wait, I could have missed out or delayed my problem. Some promises may seem to take some years but it is worth the wait. You may feel lonely at times but remember, it's worth the wait. Your finances may seem like, when God?! I know what you said! It's worth the wait. You may feel the weight … but it's worth the wait. You may feel pressed down on every side, it's worth the wait. I want this to encourage as many people as it can. I've been there; feeling forgotten, left out, mishandled, feeling as if my anointing and gifts were being pimped, uninvited, laughed at from those I didn't expect. However, the God I serve is an awesome Father. He does it big everytime!

Years ago, I lived in this apartment that a family member decided not to move into. She had already signed the lease. She asked me would I like to move in and take over the lease. I was in search so it worked out perfectly. I moved in. The next month, I went to pay the rent but the leasing agent said it was paid. The Lord told me that He was showing me favor. Every month after that for about 3 months, I was told the same thing. I told my mom that God was showing me favor. My mom wanted to be certain that it wasn't coming from my Aunt's account. To be fair, I asked my Aunt and she said no. After six months of living there, I received a check in the mail stating that i had over paid in rent so they were sending me a $1,500 check. God is faithful! It was worth the wait. I was believing God for unexpected money. He came through with the exact amount I needed. The Word was given that He was showing me favor and He did exactly what He said he would. Waiting is not easy, but is worth it. Hold fast to His promise. Waiting is the name of the game. He can do you better than any human on this earth.

I hope this chapter builds your faith up so that you stay the course. I pray you won't let the Lord go until He blesses you just like Jacob did. You may not understand His plan in this moment, but you will. I can't stress enough … stay the course. It'll be well worth the wait. The Lord blessed me well in my first salon. My next set of instructions the Lord told me was that He was doing it again. Here I am like, Lord, what are you up to now? That location had run its course and I was holding on for dear life. The longer I stayed (disobedience), the longer I was upholding my next. I got so many signs to move. I was comfortable in what the Lord had already established. I was stuck in not knowing when to move or trying to find the perfect time to move. I started rehearsing my victories. I stared the planning the process because where I was tied to being dried up. He was doing a new thing. I began to sell everything. I made plans to take over the lease at this Barber/Salon because the owner wanted to transition out. The door was a blessing although the transition didn't happen. I had favor with the owner. He told me I didn't have to pay booth rent and he poured so much into me. He pretty much fed me everyday. I think we were the company that each needed for that season. It felt like a season of rest. The load wasn't on me as far as ownership. The only thing I had to do was show up. I had taken so many customers in my last season and I was a little burnt out. This was my opportunity to rest and prepare for the new thing. Thing's began to shift again tremendously. I was blessed with a new car and moved into my new place. Favor surrounded me as a shield. As I was getting settled into my new place, this guy reached out to me saying someone tossed my name in the wind. He stated he was looking for someone to sow into that wanted to start a business. I began to tell him my vision and he immediately started the search for the location. He called me everyday to either update me or ask to meet to look at a building. In the midst of the search, my car was accidentally repossessed. The guy called me as usual and asked me to go look at a building because he was on vacation visiting family. I was to embarrassed to tell him about my car situation. One, I thought he wouldn't believe me. Secondly, I didn't want to be judged. He kept prowling as he knew something was wrong but I was determined not to tell him. The car company wanted me to pay the towing fees although it was their fault. The guy ended up saying out of the blue, "What's wrong with your car?" With my mouth wide open, I couldn't lie. He then asked me how much. At that point, I was in tears. I told him what had happened. He asked me to send him the info and he would pay everything to get it back. I had to wait after the holiday to get it back. He sent me a copy of the receipt to show me he had paid it. Of course, I'm jumping up at this time in such gratefulness. When the gentlemen got back from vacation, he came over to check my car out to see if it needed any maintenance. He realized that I needed a tire. He demanded that I come ride with him and he took me to order 4 brand new tires. He said: "Now, we can focus on finding a building". Not even a few days later ,he called to ask what type of salon furniture I wanted. At this point, he had done enough so I felt like I would just shoot for furniture that was very reasonable. I sent him pics of deals for styling chairs that ranged from $99-$139. He said no and divulged that he found this website with more expensive furniture. The ones he was choosing were $400 a piece. He asked if I wanted quality. I knew I wanted quality, but I also knew how to work with what I have. The Lord was taking me higher without settling. He purchased everything in the salon plus paid all the bills in business and in my personal life. I was blown away. Here you go again God, raising up beautiful angels on earth to bless me. He never complained about what he would do for me. He paid everything for 8 years straight without missing a beat in my business and my personal life. The Lord is awesome! He made me his lady and the rest was history. Again, he never complained. Remember, the Lord told me He was doing a new thing. He did it again and again! It was all worth the wait!

RESOURCES

Holy Bible, King James Version (KJV)

ABOUT THE AUTHOR

Martina Sims

Martina is a very passionate woman of faith, an entrepreneur, and a women's empowerment advocate with over 20 years of experience in the beauty industry. A South Carolina Native, she has dedicated her life to inspiring others, especially women to embrace their inner and outer beauty, strength, and potential. She has worked with women from all works of life, listening to their stories, sharing wisdom, and helping them see the power within themselves. Her salons were more than just a place for beauty. It has always been a safe space for transformation, conversation, and confidence-building, driven by a deep belief that every woman deserves to feel seen, heard, and celebrated. She uses her platform to uplift others through mentorship, motivational speaking, and community events. She believes in community. *"We need each other more than we realize."* Her journey is one of resilience, compassion, and purpose. She continues to be a shining light for women seeking to rediscover their worth and walk boldly in their truth.

www.ingramcontent.com/pod-product-compliance
Lightning Source LLC
LaVergne TN
LVHW052048070526
838201LV00086B/5109